The True Story of the Quest for America's Biggest Bones

THOMAS JEFFERSON and the MAMMOTH HUNT

Written by CARRIE CLICKARD Illustrated by NANCY CARPENTER

A Paula Wiseman Book · Simon & Schuster Books for Young Readers
New York London Toronto Sydney New Delhi

IN THE NEW WORLD, CALLED AMERICA, big changes were a-brewing.
Independence was declared with bold hurrahs and ballyhooing!

"This new land is so amazing! There are crops and game galore!
You want mountains? These are purple! There are rivers by the score!
We're still fighting with the British, but it's only been a year.
Come and join our brave new nation; things are better over here!"

In King Louis's court in Paris,
    Count Buffon was one smart man
    who had studied all the species known,
    since life on Earth began.
In his book he claimed the New World
    was a chilly, swampy place,
    filled with puny, scrawny creatures,
    every species, breed, and race.

"Utter nonsense!" cried Tom Jefferson.
"Our land is big and strong.
I will gather all the
facts to prove your
theory's simply wrong!"

So he set out on a tour to measure
everything Virginian: every mouse
and moose and mountain.

He would change the count's opinion!

"Here's a list of all our
great state has.

Dear Count,
please take a look. . . ."

Count Buffon? He didn't answer.

And he didn't change his book.

Thomas called on every hunter and
explorer he could find:

"Send me anything you stumble on to
change Count Buffon's mind!"

People sent him skins from wolverines
and panthers, sleek and scary.

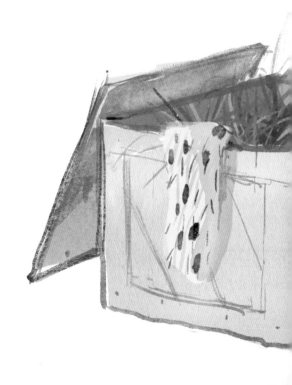

He once got a pair
of grizzly bears—
big but ordinary.

Then one day the mail deliveryman brought Thomas a surprise:
a strange pair of prehistoric claws—*three times* a lion's size!
Thomas wrote a speech about the claws, which made a huge impression
at the Philosophical Society's next monthly session.

"Now, I can't describe the creature since I only have three fossils, but I think it was a lion, and I'm sure it was COLOSSAL!" He held up the massive thighbone and the room was hushed in awe. "I have called it *megalonyx*, a Greek word that means 'great claw.'"

When more bones had been uncovered,
what Tom found surprised them all.
  Not a lion but a sloth—and one that grew to ten feet tall!
  And to honor Tom's discovery, they held a ceremony
where they named the giant sloth

the *Megalonyx jeffersonii.*

Back in France,
at his museum, Count
Buffon gave one small *tut*.

"You have found a giant sloth?
That would be quite impressive.
BUT *our* elephants are taller.
And so is *our* giraffe."

Histoire Naturelle by Moi

"This sloth is all you
have to prove your point?
Don't make me laugh."

The Society held a meeting. "We can't let our Tom fall short!
What's the biggest thing you've ever seen? Each one of you report!"
Mr. Franklin had a giant tooth—six pounds or more in size.
And George Washington once saw a skull that came up to his eyes!

There was one man, Mr. Wistar, who had bones right at his house
that would make a normal elephant look like a teeny mouse!

Tom collected teeth and jawbones, every bone someone would share.
Then he sent them with a note: "Dear Count, I dare you to compare!"

"Sacré bleu!" the count wrote back. "I do not know what all the fuss is. You've just sent me teeth from elephants and hippopotamuses. We have live ones. You do not. So we are bigger, *oui*? But when you discover something better, please feel free to write again."

"Write him back?" poor Thomas cried.
"I'll give that Count Buffon a letter!
How about the letter *O*?
The name 'Buffoon' would suit him better."

Tom remembered Mr. Wistar's tales of bones
    at Big Bone Lick.
They've got piles of tusks and teeth and ribs—
    just go and take your pick.
Tom was busy with elections.
    Someone else would have to go.
"I will send a note with Daniel Boone.
    He's headed west, I know."

Daniel hiked off to Big Bone Lick with Tom's letter in his vest,
gave the note to Dr. Goforth, then continued farther west.
Tom wrote: "I hear you've uncovered an enormous mammoth beast.
Any bones that you can spare, please box them up and ship them east!"

Thomas waited. Thomas wondered.
He kept checking on his mail.
But no mammoth bones arrived.
Was his great plan about to fail?

Then good news came from New York. Another mammoth had been found!
Would somebody come and get it out of Farmer Masten's ground?

"I'll invite Buffon to see it!"
But the count was laid to rest.
And his book still sold like
hotcakes!
Tom could not give up his
quest.

Tom had lots of work to do—he'd been elected president.
There were laws to make and land to buy and battles to prevent.
The Louisiana Purchase was new land he'd bought from France.
Thomas wanted it explored, and he knew just who'd take the chance.
Mr. Clark and Mr. Lewis—they'd be perfect for the task!
"Map it all and send reports back. Oh! And one more thing I'd ask:

Keep your eyes peeled for my mammoths!

"There could be herds way out West.
I'll be glad to get more fossils, but a live one would be best!"
From Kentucky to the ocean the explorers trekked and charted,
but they never found a mammoth. Tom tried not to be downhearted.

Back up north at Masten's farm, there were some problems with the dig.

Charles Peale had never tried to move a skeleton so big.
Water poured into the hole, no matter how fast people bailed.
So they had to send a letter saying, "Sorry, sir, we've failed."

Thomas wasn't giving up.

"How can we fix this, Mr. Peale?"

Mr. Peale said, "It sounds funny, but I think we need a wheel."

Tom sent money.

Tom sent workers.

And the waterwheel was built.

It scooped water from the hole so
bones stopped sinking in the silt.

Weeks and weeks passed while they labored,
stopping just to eat and sleep.

When they finished, their reward?
A stack of bones *three hundred deep*!

They packed boxes. They packed barrels.
Shipped the president a herd!

Tom said, "Bring them in the White House!"
No one dared to say a word.

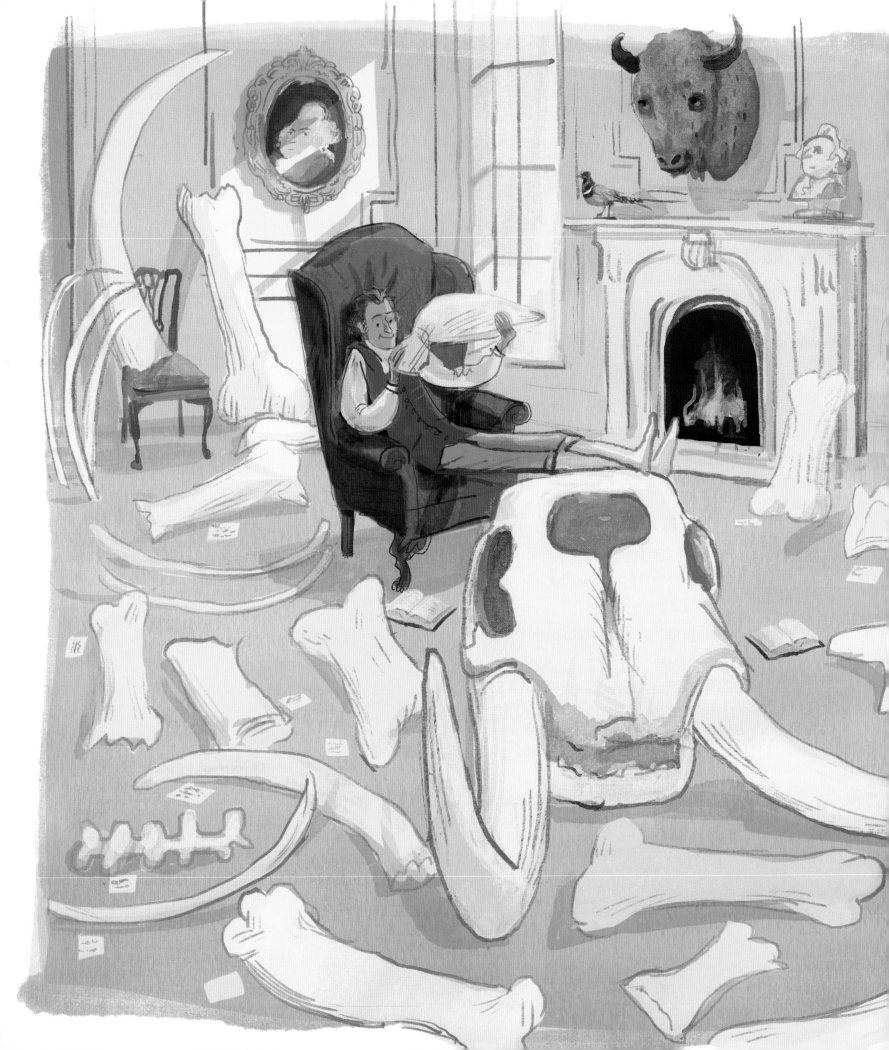

It was time to tag and sort them,
not just leave bones in a heap.
They marked some for Peale's
museum and a few for Tom to keep.

And the bones they had left over?
Tom knew just what he should do.
If America had her mammoth—
well then, France should have one too!
So they shipped the bones to Paris,

where they put them
on display:

The American
Woolly Mammoth
Courtesy of Thomas J.

AUTHOR'S NOTE

The hunt for America's mammoth began in 1705 with the discovery of a giant tooth along the banks of the Hudson River, not far from Masten's farm, where Charles Willson Peale helped dig up the first complete mammoth skeleton almost a century later. The five-pound tooth rolled downhill and landed at the feet of a Dutch tenant farmer, who promptly traded it to a local politician for a glass of rum. The politician made the tooth a gift to Lord Cornbury, the governor of New York. The tooth quickly became the talk of the town.

Based on the size of bones discovered near the tooth, Massachusetts poet Edward Taylor imagined a creature that stood sixty or seventy feet tall. (A bit of an exaggeration, since the largest mammoths were only about fifteen feet high.) Still, Taylor's slightly silly poetry about "ribs like rafters" and arms "like limbs of trees" caught the imagination of the American public.

Soon everyone was talking about this "incognitum"—the unknown animal. The Puritan minister Cotton Mather boasted that this New World giant would make Goliath look like a pygmy. Benjamin Franklin studied bones on display in London and brought a thighbone back to the Philosophical Society. During a break in the fighting of the Revolutionary War, George Washington took a sleigh full of his officers to see some of these huge bones, one a skull that was taller than a man. Scientists and amateurs alike started collecting bones, trying to build an entire skeleton.

It was only natural that Thomas Jefferson, a man of enormous scientific curiosity, would hear about these strange bones. He exchanged letters with scientists, explorers, soldiers, and kings, trying to solve this "mammoth mystery." Perhaps we should say "mastodon mystery," because we now know the bones they were uncovering actually belonged to American mastodons. At the time, however, they called the enormous beast "mammoth," and the name stuck. But then Georges-Louis Leclerc, Comte de Buffon, the French naturalist and one of the most widely read authors of the time, published a volume of his *Histoire naturelle*. He stated that "an unprolific land" caused species in the New World to become puny and "degenerate."

Jefferson was outraged. Surely no one would believe this! And yet the insulting theory was not only rapidly accepted, it was expanded. Respected writers like Abbé Raynal claimed Europeans who emigrated to America would become degenerate and so would their children. Books on American degeneracy were translated from French into a score of languages, including German, Dutch, and English. Even American newspapers like the Massachusetts *Gazette*, the Pennsylvania *Packet*, and the Maryland *Herald* spread Buffon's outrageous claims.

If people stopped emigrating to America, what would become of their young nation? Clearly, finding a complete mammoth skeleton was no longer a matter of personal curiosity for Jefferson, it was a matter of national importance. He set out to find something big enough to prove Count Buffon wrong. Thus began the famous exchange of letters (and bones) between Jefferson and Buffon. Those primary source letters were the inspiration for the imagined conversations you've read in this book. And while we've used lighthearted banter to amuse the reader, the need to disprove the "degeneracy theory" was of very serious concern to many in America. Thankfully, with help from Daniel Boone (who never wore that raccoon cap, although we all recognize him by it), explorers Lewis and Clark, and Dr. Goforth of Big Bone Lick, Jefferson succeeded. The fact that he did so while also being governor of Virginia, writing the Declaration of Independence, and serving as both vice president and president of the United States is astonishing.

Still, as bright as Jefferson painted America's future and as hard as he worked to prove it, there were also mighty clouds on the horizon. The despicable practice of slave ownership stained his path and many others in this book: George Washington, Daniel Boone, William Clark, and Charles W. Peale (although he later became an ardent abolitionist). Because of this, while we know some early Americans of color took part in the mammoth skeleton hunt, we have little more than names to remember them by. What did Moses Williams, slave, freedman, artist, think about while he was helping assemble the mammoth? Did Jupiter and Robert Hemings find Jefferson's quest for bones foolish or fascinating? What did York feel when he stood beneath the massive ribs and tusks at Big Bone Lick with Lewis and Clark? Our history would be so much richer if we could hear their voices.

This book is dedicated to those lost voices and all the voices yet to be heard.

—C. C.

Who's Who

Daniel Boone An expert tracker, hunter, and soldier, Daniel helped to explore the state of Kentucky and became famous for his courage and his raccoon-skin cap. (The hat was only added by storytellers. Daniel never wore one.) Because Daniel knew the woods and trails so well, Thomas Jefferson chose him to carry a letter about mammoth bones to Big Bone Lick in Kentucky.

Count Buffon (Georges-Louis Leclerc) A famous French scientist and writer, Count Buffon studied everything from astronomy to physics, but he is best known for his work in natural history, the study of animals and plants. The thirty-six books that make up Count Buffon's encyclopedia of "natural history" include a theory that America's weather was too wet and hot, which made its animals small and weak.

Benjamin Franklin A founding father of the United States, Ben was a printer, writer, inventor, and scientist. He helped write the Declaration of Independence and the Constitution of the United States. Ben formed the "Philosophical Society," a club where scholars and scientists shared ideas and news from around the world. This is the club where Thomas Jefferson made his famous speech on the giant sloth—the *Megalonyx jeffersonii*.

Thomas Jefferson Tom was the governor of Virginia, the author of the Declaration of Independence, and the third president of the United States. He was interested in math, science, and philosophy. Because of his interest in dinosaur bones and fossils, Tom is known as one of the fathers of American paleontology—the study of fossil plants and animals.

Meriwether Lewis and William Clark Soldiers and trackers, Lewis and Clark were hired by Thomas Jefferson to explore the Louisiana Purchase—820,000 square miles of land that America bought from France. They started the Corps of Discovery, a group of men who spent three years mapping and recording all the plants, animals, and people they met. While they traveled, Thomas Jefferson asked them to watch for any herds of "live mammoths."

Farmer (John) Masten John Masten grew wheat and calico corn on his farm in Shawangunk, New York. His workers were digging up "marl" (lime-rich mud that was mixed with manure for fertilizer) when giant bones were discovered. These bones would help make the first complete mammoth skeleton in America.

Charles Willson Peale A talented painter, Charles opened a gallery filled with portraits of famous people like George Washington, Benjamin Franklin, and Thomas Jefferson. When he was hired to draw the mammoth bones dug up at Big Bone Lick, Charles added the drawings to his gallery along with a few bones. This was the beginning of the Philadelphia Museum. Thomas Jefferson sent Charles to New York to help dig up the mammoth skeleton on Farmer Masten's land.

George Washington George was the first president of the United States and a good friend of Thomas Jefferson. They worked together and were both members of the Philosophical Society. During a break in the fighting in America's Revolutionary War, George took his officers to see mammoth bones.

Caspar Wistar Caspar was a doctor who taught anatomy (the study of animal bodies and skeletons) at the University of Pennsylvania. He was a member of the Philosophical Society, along with Benjamin Franklin, George Washington, and many others. He helped Thomas Jefferson identify the giant sloth bones and also sorted the mammoth bones collected from Big Bone Lick.

What's What

Big Bone Lick A marshy area in northern Kentucky where prehistoric animals gathered to eat plants and the salty clay. Many mammoths were trapped and died in these bogs. Their giant bones were seen by Native Americans and European settlers who came to Big Bone Lick to gather salt. Thomas Jefferson sent Daniel Boone to Big Bone Lick in hopes of finding a mammoth skeleton.

Botanical Gardens (Jardin des Plantes) In 1635 King Louis XIII's doctor planted an herb garden. By 1640 this grew into the "Jardin des Plantes," a garden where scientists could study plants, and people could come to see them displayed. Count Buffon became the director in 1739. The Jardin des Plantes is still part of France's Museum of Natural History today.

Louisiana Purchase A part of North America that ran from the state of Montana in the north to Louisiana in the south. In 1803 Thomas Jefferson bought the land from France in a deal called the "Louisiana Purchase." He sent Lewis and Clark to map this land and write down all that they learned about the plants, animals, and people that lived on it.

Mammoth A prehistoric mammal very much like an elephant only with shorter ears and shaggy fur. Mammoths could grow up to fifteen feet tall and could weigh more than twelve thousand pounds. Mastodons are slightly smaller than mammoths, with shorter legs and lower, flatter heads. The bones of the animal Jefferson called a mammoth actually belonged to an American mastodon.

Masten's Farm (Masten's Meadow) A wheat and Indian corn farm in Shawangunk, New York (about eighty-five miles north of New York City). Farm workers were digging up "marl" (lime-rich mud that was mixed with manure for fertilizer) when the giant mammoth bones were discovered.

Philosophical Society (American Philosophical Society) A club for scholars, scientists, and thinkers, founded by Benjamin Franklin in Philadelphia in 1743. Many famous Americans were members, including George Washington, John Adams, and Thomas Jefferson. The Society still exists today and you can visit its museum.

Peale Museum The first museum in America. Charles Peale started with a single room full of paintings, then added fossils and all sorts of natural history exhibits, from butterflies to mammoths. Peale's collections are still on display in museums today.

White House The house where the president of the United States lives and works.

Further Reading

About Thomas Jefferson

Chew, Elizabeth V. *Thomas Jefferson: A Day at Monticello.* New York: Harry N. Abrams, 2014.

Fleming, Candace. *A Big Cheese for the White House: The True Tale of a Tremendous Cheddar.* New York: Square Fish, 2004.

Fradin, Dennis Brindell. *Who Was Thomas Jefferson?* New York: Grosset & Dunlap, 2003.

Kalman, Maira. *Thomas Jefferson: Life, Liberty and the Pursuit of Everything.* New York: Nancy Paulsen Books, 2014.

Kerley, Barbara. *Those Rebels, John and Tom.* New York: Scholastic, 2012.

Rosenstock, Barb. *Thomas Jefferson Builds a Library.* Honesdale, PA: Calkins Creek, 2013.

About Big Bone Lick, Peale's Museum, and Mammoth Bones

Giblin, James Cross. *The Mystery of the Mammoth Bones.* New York: HarperCollins, 1999.

Morrison, Taylor. *Mastodon Mystery.* Boston: HMH Books for Young Readers, 2006.

Wilson, Janet. *The Ingenious Mr. Peale: Painter, Patriot and Man of Science.* New York: Atheneum, 1996.

Primary Sources

"In America, therefore, animated Nature is weaker, less active, and . . . the numbers of species is not only fewer, but all the animals are much smaller than those of the Old Continent."—*Histoire naturelle* (Vol. 5), Georges-Louis Leclerc, Comte de Buffon,1766

". . . that insects, reptiles, and all the animals which wallow in the mire, whose blood is watery, and which multiply in corruption, are larger and more numerous in the low, moist, and marshy lands of the New Continent."—*Histoire naturelle* (Vol. 5), Georges-Louis Leclerc, Comte de Buffon, 1766

"Monsr. de Buffon . . . has advanced a theory in general very degrading to America . . . an opinion which I think not founded in fact."—"From Thomas Jefferson to Ezra Stiles, 10 June 1784," *Founders Online,* National Archives, last modified December 28, 2016, http://founders.archives.gov/documents/Jefferson/01-07-02-0251.

"I thought the bones of a Tremendious animal of the Clawed kind lately found in a Cave . . . might afford you some amusement."—"To Thomas Jefferson from John Stuart, 11 April 1796," *Founders Online,* National Archives, last modified April 12, 2018, http://founders.archives.gov/documents/Jefferson/01-29-02-0043.

"Its bulk entitles it to give to our animal the name of the Great-claw, or Megalonyx."—"From Thomas Jefferson to David Rittenhouse, 3 July 1796," *Founders Online,* National Archives, last modified December 28, 2016, http://founders.archives.gov/documents/Jefferson/01-29-02-0104.

". . . he was *more* than three times as large as the lion:"—Memoir on the Megalonyx, [10 February 1797]," *Founders Online,* National Archives, last modified December 28, 2016, http://founders.archives.gov/documents/Jefferson/01-29-02-0232.

"I received your favor by Colo. Boon . . . to procure you those Curiosities you want."— To Thomas Jefferson from George Rogers Clark, 20 February 1782," *Founders Online,* National Archives, last modified December 28, 2016, http://founders.archives.gov/documents/Jefferson/01-06-02-0150.

"Other objects worthy of notice will be . . . animals of the country generally not known in the U.S. and the remains and accounting *of any which may be deemed rare or extinct.*"—Jefferson's instructions to Meriwether Lewis & the Corps of Discovery, 20 June 1803

"Have you received any accounts respecting the large bones which have lately been found up the North River in the State of New York . . ."—"To Thomas Jefferson from Caspar Wistar, 19 October 1800," *Founders Online,* National Archives, last modified December 28, 2016, http://founders.archives.gov/documents/Jefferson/01-32-02-0138.

"The pits dug to get the bones are now full of water, and one of them 12 feet deep . . . it appears an Herculean task to explore the bottom where the remainder of the bones are . . ."—"To Thomas Jefferson from Charles Willson Peale, 29 June 1801," *Founders Online,* National Archives, last modified December 28, 2016, http://founders.archives.gov/documents/Jefferson/01-34-02-0378.

"The Idea instantly occurred of a chain of Buckets carried round an axis, pouring the lifted Water into a Trough communicating to the Basin."—"To Thomas Jefferson from Charles Willson Peale, 11 October 1801," *Founders Online,* National Archives, last modified December 28, 2016, http://founders.archives.gov/documents/Jefferson/01-35-02-0355.

"The bones are spread in a large room, where you can work at your leisure."—"From Thomas Jefferson to Caspar Wistar, 20 March 1808," *Founders Online,* National Archives, last modified December 28, 2016, http://founders.archives.gov/documents/Jefferson/99-01-02-7673.

"It is a precious collection, consisting of upwards of 300 bones . . . there are 4 pieces of the head, one very clean & distinctly presenting the whole face of the animal."—"From Thomas Jefferson to Caspar Wistar, 20 March 1808," *Founders Online,* National Archives, last modified December 28, 2016, http://founders.archives.gov/documents/Jefferson/99-01-02-7673.

"If my recollection does not deceive me, the collection of the remains of the Mammoth possessed by the Cabinet of Natural history at Paris, is not very copious . . . the enclosed catalogue of specimens which I am now able to place at the disposal of the National Institute."—"From Thomas Jefferson to Bernard Germain Etienne de La Ville-sur-Illon, Comte de Lacépède, 14 July 1808," *Founders Online,* National Archives, last modified December 28, 2016, http://founders.archives.gov/documents/Jefferson/99-01-02-8319.

FOR ALL THE CURIOUS MINDS WHO WILL ONE DAY BE
PRESIDENTS OR PALEONTOLOGISTS OR BOTH—C. C.

FOR MAEVE AND GARETH—N. C.

The publisher gratefully acknowledges Peter S. Onuf, Thomas Jefferson professor emeritus of
history at the University of Virginia, for reviewing this book for accuracy.

SIMON & SCHUSTER BOOKS FOR YOUNG READERS

An imprint of Simon & Schuster Children's Publishing Division

1230 Avenue of the Americas, New York, New York 10020

Text copyright © 2019 by Carrie Clickard

Illustrations copyright © 2019 by Nancy Carpenter

SIMON & SCHUSTER BOOKS FOR YOUNG READERS is a trademark of Simon & Schuster, Inc.

For information about special discounts for bulk purchases, please contact

Simon & Schuster Special Sales at 1-866-506-1949 or business@simonandschuster.com.

The Simon & Schuster Speakers Bureau can bring authors to your live event. For more information or to book an event,

contact the Simon & Schuster Speakers Bureau at 1-866-248-3049 or visit our website at www.simonspeakers.com.

The text for this book was set in Adobe Garamond Pro.

The illustrations for this book were rendered digitally.

Manufactured in China

1018 SCP

First Edition

2 4 6 8 10 9 7 5 3 1

Library of Congress Cataloging-in-Publication Data

Names: Clickard, Carrie (Carrie L.), author. | Carpenter, Nancy, illustrator.

Title: Thomas Jefferson and the mammoth hunt : the true story of the quest for America's biggest bones / Carrie Clickard ; illustrated by Nancy Carpenter.

Description: 1st edition. | New York : Simon & Schuster Books for Young Readers, [2017] |

"A Paula Wiseman Book." | Audience: Ages 4–8 | Audience: K to grade 3

Identifiers: LCCN 2014050018 | ISBN 9781481442688 (hardcover) | ISBN 9781481442695 (eBook)

Subjects: LCSH: Jefferson, Thomas, 1743–1826—Juvenile literature. | Buffon, Georges Louis Leclerc, comte de,

1707–1788—Juvenile literature. | Woolly mammoth—Juvenile literature. | Mammals, Fossil—United States—Juvenile literature. | Natural history—

United States—Juvenile literature. | United States—History—1783–1815—Juvenile literature. Classification: LCC QH31.B88 C55 2017 | DDC 508.0973—dc23

LC record available at https://lccn.loc.gov/2014050018